1996

Sharon —

This book just
looked like it belonged
to you, my friend.

Love,
Arlene

Your Hand in Mine

Other titles in the
Treasures of Inspiration series

FROM THE HEART
Poems of Praise and Thanks

THE GUIDING LIGHT
Poems of Faith and Hope

HOPE IN DARKNESS
Poems of Sorrow and Comfort

YOUR HAND IN MINE

Poems of Love and Friendship

Antioch Publishing Company
Yellow Springs, Ohio 45387
0-89954-778-8

Printed in Hong Kong through Bookbuilders Ltd

CONTENTS

YOUR HAND IN MINE
Patricia Hadgifotis

Arise, My love, My lovely one,
Arise and come with Me.
For I go to the mountain tops,
To go where I can see.

Come with Me now, arise, My love,
Come, place your hand in Mine.
And I will lead you safe at last
Through the troubled times.

Arise, My love, My lovely one,
Arise and come with Me.
Follow in My footsteps
And I'll lead you to safety.

Through troubles, toils and tears, My love,
That you thought I did not see,
I was with you all the time, My love,
And now I've set you free.

Arise, My love, My lovely one,
Arise and come with Me,
For I go to the mountain tops,
To go where you can see.

GOD'S KIND OF LOVE
Glenda Mitchel Palmer

Not a promise of summer sun
Without the winter rain;
Not always a promise of pleasure,
Sometimes a promise of pain;
But love is worth whatever the price
It costs to keep it growing;
For love is the only lasting truth,
The only promise worth knowing.

PROMISE OF PEACE
Marilyn Ashcroft

Have you ever wandered
By a quiet rippling stream,
Seen the beauty all around
And allowed yourself to dream?
Relaxed in perfect stillness
And the only sounds you hear
Are those which God intended
And you feel his presence near.
And as you allow His love
Quietly to fill your heart
You feel the tension slipping,
And the peace He can impart
Comes stealing in so softly
As He bids your cares be gone.
You hear a gentle whisper,
Won't you trust Me as the one
Who gives to you a peace more deep
Than you have ever known?
Just let me take your burdens,
For you are My very own.

TOGETHER
Geoffrey A. Dudley

Here where the valley runs down to the sea
Let me be spending a lifetime with you,
Together in gladness, together in pain.
There are so many things we could do
Whether the weather was sunshine or rain.
If you won't spend your lifetime with me,
Perhaps you can spare me a moment or two
Here where the pine trees sweep down to the sea.

'GOD IS NEARER TO US THAN OUR OWN SOUL': JULIAN OF NORWICH

Dorothy Munt

Jesus, nearer than my soul,
Closer than my breath of life,
Come and guide me through the dark,
Guard me in my earthly strife.

Christ, who in Your darkest night,
Longed for God and human touch,
Show us, in our lonely hour,
How your dear heart aches for such.

Shall I then, Your sinful child,
Faint, and think I walk alone?
No, I will abide in Him,
He in me, and we are one.

THAT SPECIAL GIFT
Marilyn Ashcroft

Friendship is something which money can't buy
For its value just cannot be measured.
More precious than jewels, or silver, or gold,
This friendship must simply be treasured.
You find that it grows even richer with time,
Being born out of laughter and tears,
For sharing the heartaches which life brings our way,
Bringing comfort to cope with our fears.
The knowledge that somebody knows how you feel
Without ever a word being spoken,
Those feelings which lie so deep down inside,
Knowing confidence will not be broken,
For the bond with which friendship is circled
Is much stronger than sometimes we know,
For in riding the storms out together
We'll be helping each other to grow.
Yes, real friendship is something quite special,
Graciously sent from the Father above,
Bound so closely with trust and affection,
Reflecting His care and sharing His love.

PURE LOVE
Hazel Bishop

Pure, precious love so rich, so warm,
Why has it come to me?
I'm lonely, cold and empty –
However can it be?

What pure delight I find in Him
Who died upon the tree.
His love is all-consuming,
And given to me free.

The lonely, cold and empty days
Are passing from my view,
Because the love of Jesus
Envelops like the dew.

No need to go on searching now,
I've come alive in Him.
His shining light is on me,
And never will go dim.

O precious Saviour, love divine,
That reaches even me.
Forever in Your arms I'll stay,
So loved, so safe, so free.

SHARING
Linda Butters

Be glad that you are living,
Be glad the sun still shines,
Be glad that you are giving,
To friends along the way,
Making sure you're brightening up
Someone else's day.
Keeping blues away,
Keeping tears at bay.
Go along life's weary road
And face each day that comes.
Just remember you are helping
Someone share the load.

A CHILD'S PRAYER
Kevin Dean

Deep in my heart, O Lord, I know,
You live and speak to me.
God of the sun, the moon and stars,
God of the earth and sea.
You made the angels, you made mankind,
A long, long time ago;
You made them beautiful, you made them good,
And you have told me so.
Deep in my heart, O whisper to me,
That You have come to save;
When I am frightened, when I am weak,
Lord, make me strong and brave.
Tell me, dear Lord, how much You love me.
And may I remember, too,
God of my heart, my mind and strength,
To say, sometimes, I love You.

AN IRISH LEGEND
Thomas Foy

The door's on the latch since twilight gathered,
A candle gleams in each window-pane,
Perhaps tonight if the inns are crowded,
They'll shelter here from the wind and rain.

'Tis but a tale, an Irish legend,
Ever repeated each Christmas night,
And children listen in wide-eyed wonder,
Beside the turf-fire's flickering light.

The first latch lifted, so runs the legend,
If children love them, 'tis there they'll stay,
And with the dawning of Christmas morning
They'll leave a present and steal away.

Soon Mary enters with gentle Joseph
To bring each sleeper some Christmas joy,
And Christmas morning beneath each pillow
Will nestle softly that longed-for toy.

SAFE IN THE ARMS OF JESUS
Lyn Bevan

Safe in the arms of Jesus,
Safe in the arms of a friend,
Safe in the arms of Jesus,
His love it has no end.

I know He is there beside me
In all that I say and do;
I know He is there to guide me,
His love will see me through.

Go forth, go forth with Jesus,
There is no need to doubt;
Have faith in Him who loves you,
That's what life's all about.

Life is a long, long journey,
Don't travel it alone;
You have a friend to guide you,
One you can call your own.

Be guided by His wisdom,
By guided by His power,
Life will have real, true meaning
In every waking hour.

Seek and you're sure to find Him,
Knock and He'll hear your call;
Then you'll be ever guided,
Onwards unto your goal.

A NEW BEGINNING
Sister M. Francis

I've come to You, dear Jesus,
All I want to say,
To ask You for forgiveness
When I let You down today.
I now renew my promise
To please You more each day
By trying to be more humble
In a simple Christ-like way.

CAN YOU SEE?
Marilyn Ashcroft

How can I see Jesus
As I live my daily life?
How can I see Jesus
When all around is strife?

Can you see that woman
As she struggles on the bus,
Weighted down with shopping bags,
Children kicking up a fuss?

Can you see that neighbour
Who needs a helping hand?
She cannot do her garden
For she can hardly stand.

Can you see that little child
Who's trying not to cry?
He's got no one to play with.
He's really very shy.

Can you see that patient
Who lies so ill in bed,
Feeling quite forgotten?
How many tears they shed.

Can you see that coloured boy?
He is looking, oh, so sad.
No one seems to talk to him,
But he's just a little lad.

Can't you see the Saviour
In someone else's need?
Can't you see the Saviour
With feet and hands that bleed?

Take a look around you
And hear His heartfelt plea:
'If you do it for the least of these,
You do it as for Me.'

REVELATION
E..M. Ashton

As the mirror of Your words shows my reflection,
I gaze on imperfection,
And wonder why You Love me, Lord.

My thoughtless disobedience is revealed,
Nothing concealed from Your omniscience.
Your spirit woos in silence.
Restored, Your smile is upon me,
And I know You love me, Lord.

HEAVENLY SILENCE
Jackie Finch

No need for words – He knows.
His will be done – not thine.
When all around seems desolate
He gives His love divine.
He will not let thee fall;
His hand is there to guide.
If thou shouldst ever think Him gone
He'll still be at thy side.
Although thy spirit breaks
When striving for thy goal,
Think thou of Him – He understands
And cares for every soul.

PEBBLES
Anthony Foy

As passing pebbles in the sea
Meet, and are parted instantly,
So for a moment met have we –
The wave-tossed of humanity.
Yet in that moment I have seen
A thousand joys that might have been,
And are not, and can never be,
So long as motion stirs the sea:
Joys to dream, but not to keep,
A thousand joys to make us weep;
Joys dim-seen through blinding tears,
Clutched at through the mists of years;
Half-seen joys from which we learn
God's own beauty to discern;
Joys that bring before our eyes
Sweet visionings of Paradise;
Joys that this short life transcend,
Joys too great to brook an end;
The thousand joys that soon will be,
When death has stilled the raging sea.

But whilst we're tossed by every tide,
And all our hopes seem swept aside,
Through every peril to the end,
I am your brother and your friend;
Till, cast up on the eternal shore,
We pebbles meet – to part no more!

THREE KINDS OF LOVE
Frances Fry

Love that takes
Is the love that breaks.
Love that ties
Is the love that dies.
But love that gives
Is the love that lives.

MY BABY
Sheelagh FitzGerald

Born of my pleasure and my pain
You lie there,
Small, innocent, perfect.
Your little body created by the union of two,
And from it you show – his eyes, my hands,
His brown skin, my dimples.
Yet you are unique. You have your own spirit.
I look at you with all my love,
I will care for you always, and the bond
I have with you will endure my life through.
For though you must go onward to live your life
I have given you a part of me that I cannot
Claim back.
Grow, my darling, in beauty and joy.
The privilege of sharing your growing life
Will be a happiness that no one can ever
Take away from me, no matter
What the future holds.

BLIND EYES
Marilyn Ashcroft

Once I was blind, but now I see
The wonderful things You've done for me.
Once I was lost in sorrow and shame,
Now nothing will ever be quite the same.

For love touched my life in a wonderful way,
One day as I knelt and started to pray.
I suddenly felt a burden had shifted
And in Your arms I found I was lifted.

I felt such peace flow into my soul,
And knew that I was being made whole.
For all the pressure and strain was gone.
And I knew at last a victory was won.

And now at last my arms I can raise
In love and worship, thanksgiving and praise.
And all that I owe I can never repay,
For You sought me out and showed me Your way.

TIME ENOUGH TO LOVE
Stan Irvine

It never seems there's time enough
To capture things we've lost;
We'll do that in the spring, we say,
But spring's soon turned to frost.
While in the islands of our hearts
We shed a lonely tear,
Another spring has come and gone;
We've lost another year.
But in that year we did so much!
From duties did not shirk;
We went to all our meetings
And persevered at work;
We read important books as well,
Sharpened up the mind,
And often aided charities
For each of us is kind.
We made all our obeisances
To a world of push and shove,
Yet forgot the most important thing –
To leave some time for love.

BE KIND
Thomas Foy

Sickness, sorrow, pain and trouble,
Such the lot of mortal man,
For man's nature has not altered
Since our history began.

Why must man seek man's destruction
Causing death by bomb and gas?
Life is short, and e'en earth's strongest
To his judgement soon must pass.

Why should I destroy my neighbour
Who is like unto his God?
Soon, too soon, his lifeless body
Will rest like mine beneath the sod.

So today with God my helper,
I will a little kinder be
To my neighbour; fellow-traveller
To a long eternity.

AS I AM
Shelagh Gemmel

Alone and lost
In a strange world
Of misunderstandings, misunderstood,
Hopeless and helpless,
In a tormented mind of previous times
Where nothing was good

To You I cried,
Please, look and see
Me
In all my dark despair
Me
Enslaved, my sins laid bare –
Each and every one for you to see
(Why should You care for such as me?)

You came
And I was taken up
By love
So pure and real.

You came
To take
Me
As I am –
To take me
And to heal.

My loving Lord, how can it be
That I should be so blessed,
That I should find
Such peace
Such love
Such healing
Quiet
Rest.

THE CHILD
Helen Froome

I thought that I knew my God;
I saw His guidance when I chose right from wrong;
I saw His mercy when I chose wrong from right;
I saw His compassion when I mourned;
And I saw His greatness in His creation.

But today I found His love.
A love more sweet and gentle than I thought
Such a mighty being could behold.
It was not buried deep beneath the ground,
Nor was it concealed at the highest summit;
For I found His love in the eyes of a child.

As she took my hand and knelt beside me
She smiled at me.
This tiny bundle of happiness,
So cherished and loved by the highest of all,
Smiled – upon me.

And as she spoke, she spoke with the gentleness
Of a flowing stream,
And the radiance of her countenance filled the room
As it poured into my heart.

Lord, as surely as Peter is Your rock,
So too are these tiny children Your gemstones.

Pure as diamonds,
Fresh as emeralds,
Warm as rubies.

Yet, for any of these stones, however precious,
To glisten,
They need first a light to fall upon them,
And dwell within them.

I LOVE YOU, GOD
Patricia Hadgifotis

Lost in a world falling apart,
Once I met You.
Viewed through a glass darkly,
Endeavoured to understand and follow.

I lost the way.
Once again You found me,
Undone, broken.

Granted me
Once again new hope and vision and now
Divine life with You.

THERE IS A TIME
L. MacDonald

There is a time
Between the last fall of snow
And the first flowering of spring
When the earth sighs
And the seasons hesitate.

There is a time
Between the shadows of the night
And the dawning of the day
When the moon wanes
And the sun stands still.

There is a time
Between the birth of a child
And the death of a god
When footsteps falter
And courage fails.

At such a time
Between life and death
Between hope and despair
Your hand reached out to mine
And winter became spring.

THE FACE OF CHRIST
Susan McGowan

The face of Christ looked out of the mist
Or was it my eyes wouldn't see?
No words I heard but His deep eyes spoke
As though asking something of me.

I needed to hear, but I was deaf
To the longing I could not see
Because my self seemed not to know
He was asking something of me.

But a light so soft became a fire
And my whole being warmed to see
That look of love on the face of Christ
Was requesting something of me.

Awakened by love, my soul alert
To His pleading that I would see
His face in every person I meet,
In those faces His love of me.

FRIENDSHIP
Muriel Manton

Friendship, like the frailest flower,
Must be tended with loving care.
Sheltered from the heat and shower,
Watered with raindrops rare.

Crush the petals, and the flowers will fade,
The leaves will wither and fall.
Protect the petals from the heat and shade,
Give cover from the garden wall.

The fullness of friendship will blossom in time,
Given God's time and spoken hour,
No matter in what country or clime,
The blossom will certainly flower.

NOT ALONE
Richard Merry

What – lonely? Never! Not with such a pal
To share my infant romping on the rug . . .
The affable affray to see who shall
First clinch half-Nelson or a bunny-hug.

An only child? But what did words mean then?
What pale significance attached to 'only'?
What scanty sense of isolation when
I had a friend to keep me far from lonely?

Then schoolboy days, and still my mate was there,
With backyard cricket under summer sun –
A bosom pal to sympathise and share
My loud complaints when holidays were done.

They say that menfolk seldom know the knack
Of keeping friends through life as women do.
But, all through youth and manhood, I look back
And see a first-rate buddy, ever true.

Now, with my youth a thing long since apart,
I look back on the staunchest mate I had . . .
No longer here but always in my heart:
For that good friend was none else but my Dad.

CHILDHOOD
Penelope Bryant Turk

Let us give them memories
Of apples ripe upon the trees,
Of special meals by candlelight,
Of bedtime stories told each night,
Of faith and love so strong that we
Shall give them sure security.
Who knows what in their future lies,
What chaos then might shake the skies,
But this, their gift of childhood joy,
No future power can destroy.

THE ROSE AND THE THORN
Sister Maree CHN

Together they grew on the same stem –
The white rose and the thorn.
They grew together, the love and the pain,
The suffering and the victory.
The sin of man and the love of the pure white
    rose.
Some say the thorn is a crown,
A kingly crown, a crown that holds the suffering
    of the world.
Some say that once a King wore it;
That he wore it for love –
That he wore it for me.
Together they grew, the love and the pain.
I watched the thorn twist its cruel fingers
Deep into the heart of love
And saw the tiny drops of deep red blood
Fall like dew on the white, white rose.

THE THREE CROSSES
J.E. Norman

Three crosses,
Not just one alone.
He shared
With them
The loneliness of death.

Three bodies
Taken from the trees,
Not one.
In death
With them
That they should be transformed
By love.

It is in the sharing
That He comes among us,
One with us,
Sharing
In love,
All that we are,
All that we do,
Just as we are,
Just where we are.

LOVELY ARE THE BLUE SKIES
J. Dalmain

Lovely are the blue skies
Over this green-clad earth;
Victorious, God's love flies
Ever to us, from our birth.

LIKE THINE
W. Emery

I want, dear Lord, a heart like Thine,
Compassionate and kind,
Not harsh or wayward. I would leave
All selfish thoughts behind.

I want, dear Lord, a touch like Thine,
So firm, yet gentle too.
That my life may reflect Thy love
In everything I do.

LOVE IS A GIFT
Marilyn Ashcroft

God's love is a gift, a gift so divine,
Given so freely and I know it's mine.
I don't deserve it, but Christ died for me,
Took my sins from me and then set me free.
So great is my debt I can never repay,
All I can do is to walk in His way.
The love of the Lord is the best gift of all,
Given to those who respond to His call.
This gift is so precious and it's mine to share
With all of God's children, for love means I care.

TRUE FRIEND
Sylvia Moen

When the party is over and come to an end,
Will you still be looking for that 'special friend'
Who will walk with you on life's highway
Into every new and unexplored day?

There is a friend like that, you know,
Ready and willing His love to show
To you, who look for someone to care,
A someone who's willing your life to share.

Though you can't see Him, it doesn't mean
His support isn't there, on which to lean,
For He has said He will never leave
When once you've received Him, and are freed.

Freed, from this life's earthly woe,
To move into realms which onward go,
Reducing fear and giving rest
As you trust in Him and are blessed.

For He will come and give the peace
Which is His alone to release –
And you will know, as never before,
What friendship in Him is really for.

THE GIFT
Glenda Mitchel Palmer

What lover's gift do you desire?
Red-streaked sunsets on the edge of a star?
A cascade of falling water, tied up with a
    rainbow?
Ice-crystal trees? Butterfly wings?

A sleepy breeze winking in the tornado's angry
    eye?
Laughing windchimes in the teardrop storms?
An extended hand to a drowning lamb?
For God so loved the world, He gave. . . .

LOVE BLOSSOMS
L. MacDonald

Love blossoms
On the cherry tree –
Pink and white
Against the bluest sky.

Love spreads
Its tender tendrils
Along the branches
Of the great cedar.

Love curls
Its patterned leaves
Burnished with autumn light
And finds
Its resting place
Among the calm ripples
Of the willow pond.

THE TRUE LOVER
Harold T. Pritchard

Having Thy love, I do not care, not I,
How circumstance maltreats me, gets me down;
Faith is sufficient star to travel by,
Hope is my halo, charity my crown.
Having Thy love, I do not covet wealth
Which, I observe, is not the key to pleasure,
And e'en the enviable boon of health
Is not the apex of earthly treasure.
Having Thy love, I covet but the art
To draw Thee by the magnet of my prayer,
And feel the beating of Thy mighty heart,
And know, in ecstasy, that Thou art there.

If this is falsehood, and against me proved,
Then there's no God, and no man ever loved.

THE MEETING
Susan McGowan

I met Him in the forest of my thoughts
Walking on the wind
That clothes the trees
With joy and conquest: peace was all about.

His love was in His greeting of no words
Walking on the wind
That clothes the trees
Of kindness, patience, gentleness about.

His invitation heard to share with Him,
Walking on the wind
That clothes the trees,
His trustfulness, His goodness all about.

And from the forest of my thoughts I was
Walking on the wind
That clothes the trees,
Captured by His love, the quiet all about.

One now, we share the silence of love
Borne on the wind
Away from earthbound thoughts,
Where 'Glory! Glory!' sings of who He is
And what His love is all about.

FRIENDSHIP
Joanna Monks

A friend is someone who's always there.
You may have faults but He'll always care,
And when you're down and life looks bad
He can share it with you and also be sad.
But when you're happy and life is such fun,
You can sing and dance and be out in the sun;
One good friend in the whole of your life
Can help you survive through trouble and strife,
So value a friend with all of your heart,
And don't let anything keep you apart.

COME, THE FORSAKEN
Marianne Reynolds

Come, the forsaken, the broken-hearted,
The imprisoned, the downtrodden,
Come, sing to the Lord.
Praise Him in the cities,
On the mountains, in the fields.
For He comforts the sad heart,
Strengthens the weary.
Come, praise the Lord,
From generation to generation.
For His kindness is everlasting
And He shall lead His children gently.

ON LIFE'S HIGHWAY
Meryl Tookaram

A bright smile, a friendly
Wave, can mean so very much
To someone's day.
No man is an island –
We all have highs and lows
And you can be sure
That there will be a
Day when a bright smile,
A friendly wave,
Will help to make your
Day.
We are all
Travellers
On life's great highway.

THE TRAVELLER
Kathleen Mary Unwin

A stranger I met one day
Travelling alone,
Weary and footsore and grey,
Seeking for a home.
Sad were his eyes, but sweet.
Gentle the tone of his voice when he spoke
And asked me for bread and meat.

He stayed but an hour or so,
Then said farewell.
I asked, 'Have you far to go?'
He could not tell,
Nor knew from where he came.
Save that he journeyed from place to place,
And Kindliness was his name.

ON VISITING MY FRIEND
Ettilie Wallace

I sit
At this high window,
Look down on sand and restless sea.

I hold my friend,
My slow-to-die old friend,
Her head in my lap,
She sleeps in another time.

Ocean water
Everywhere the same –
Multitudinous the patterns thrown by its waves.

WHAT IS LOVE?
Marilyn Ashcroft

Love is giving,
Love is living,
Love is taking someone's load,
Love helps them along the road.
Love is caring,
Love is sharing.
Love will seek the best for others,
Love treats everyone as brothers.

THE JOURNEY
Michael A. Rouse

When I was young You took me by the hand
And gently down life's pathways led
My wayward wandering feet where You had
   planned.

Many's the time upon a summer's day
I fain would stop, withdraw my hand,
And linger long upon that sunnier way.

Nor out of tiredness would I rest instead,
Nor seeking pleasure, would I stay,
But through mistrust of unknown ways ahead.

Hold fast my hand, and on Your pathways keep,
For Your hand is a firmer hand:
I know You'll guide my wayward feet.

When I was young You took me by the hand;
Lead me, that I may see that golden land.

GOD'S GIFTS
Eva W. Taylor

God gave us eyes that we might see
Beauty in flower, grass and tree.
Glory of sunset, splendour of storm,
Wonder of curve and line and form.
God gave us eyes that we might see
Glimpses of immortality.

God gave us ears that we might hear
Voices of loved ones, laughter clear,
Song-time of birds and murmur of bees,
Sighing of winds and shiver of trees.
God gave us ears that we might hear
Echoes of Heaven drawing near.

God gave us lips that we might say
Words full of kindness day by day,
Words which will comfort, strengthen and heal,
Those which the Father's love will reveal.
God gave us lips that we might say
Truths about Heaven on life's way.

God gave us hearts that we might care
For all His creatures, everywhere.
Those who are needy, helpless and weak,
Who for some loving friendship seek.
God gave us hearts that we might care
And, here on earth, Heaven's blessings share.

God gave us eyes, ears, lips and hearts
To find the gifts His love imparts.
To know His great salvation here
And see Him mirrored everywhere.
God gave us eyes, ears, lips and hearts –
Thus on this earth our Heaven starts.

A HAPPY HOME
Peter Fenwick

May the child laid in a manger
Find a cradle in your care,
May the man who had no place to lay His head
Find rest under your roof,
And may the spirit of the risen Christ
Fill your hearts with joy
And your home with happiness.

Designed by Bernard Higton